SCENIC WONDERS OF THE NATIONAL PARKS OF AMERICA

SCENIC WONDERS OF THE NATIONAL PARKS OF AMERICA

JAMES MURFIN

GALLERY BOOKS
An Imprint of W. H. Smith Publishers Inc.
112 Madison Avenue
New York City 10016

Endpapers *The standing rocks at Monument Valley, Utah: a place of awesome silence and immense sunsets that fill the desert sky.*

Half title page *Fiery fountain of lava from the crater of a volcano in Hawaii.*

Facing title page *Cypress grove in Yosemite Valley. Half Dome, at the head of the valley, can be seen in the background.*

Right *Close-up of rocks in Monument Valley. These rounded boulders are of sandstone.*

This book was devised and produced by Multimedia Publications (UK) Ltd.

Editor: Marilyn Inglis
Production: Arnon Orbach
Design: Terry Allen
Picture Research: Tessa Paul

First published in the United States of America 1985 by Gallery Books, an imprint of W. H. Smith Publishers Inc., 112 Madison Avenue, New York, NY 10016.

ISBN 0 8317 7708 7

Typeset by Keene Graphics Ltd, London
Origination by The Clifton Studio Ltd, London
Printed in Italy by New Interlitho SpA, Milan

CONTENTS

PREFACE

The first book I received as a gift, when a youngster, had something to do with the Seven Wonders of the World. I can still remember its size and shape and some of the illustrations. I read the book time and time again and remember carrying it with me everywhere I went. Having such a book at that age was a wonder in itself, but one with such marvelous stories about far away places was a double treat. I had only one problem: the wonders were gone, with the exception of the Pyramids and a giant statue near Thebes, none of which I was likely to see. That meant that five of the illustrations were "artist's impressions" and the stories were probably a mixture of history and fable. I was not sophisticated enough to draw the distinction, but the whole thing gave me pause.

Then for Christmas — I suppose it was my ninth or tenth year — I was given a 16mm movie projector and two films, a Walt Disney cartoon and a film called *Yosemite*. All of a sudden I realized that Yosemite was one of the *real* wonders of the world, and it was here in America, not in some far distant land. It existed, and it was older than any of the other wonders in my little book. I called it "Yose-mite" and had show after show in the darkened cellar as kids from all over my end of town came to see what I announced as "the eighth wonder of the world shown on a white-washed wall". Where else could you get a full-length feature on Yosemite, plus Mickey Mouse, all for a nickel, and, if we were lucky, a glass of apple cider tossed in by my mother.

The film was black and white, as they all were in those days, and it had titles like "El Capitan" and "Half Dome" and "Yosemite Falls." I could run it fast or slow or stop and look at one frame at a time. It was a marvel. But still, California was a place far away. My little world extended no more than three miles in any direction. That film, however, and perhaps a copy or two of *National Geographic*, set my mind awhirl with a determination to some day see my "eighth wonder." Thirty-eight years later, I did. I was not disappointed. Yosemite was not the Hanging Gardens of Babylon or the Colossus of Rhodes, nor was it man-made, but it over shadowed all of them in beauty — even the "artist's impressions."

In the intervening years, national parks became very real places for me, and some of them my ninth and tenth wonders, until finally the wonders in the old book faded from memory. I had the good fortune to spend eighteen years of my career with the National Park Service, during which time I saw Yellowstone and Canyon de Chelly and the Grand Canyon and dozens of other places that were millions of years old. And I remembered a statement in an old encyclopedia that sort of summed up my earlier questions about "wonders." "How many modern wonders of art, science and invention," it said, "are likely to survive a thousand years and more, when fame today is as rapidly lost as it is acquired and miracles of achievement occur so often that they have ceased to be miracles?"

Previous pages Atlantic fog in the fir trees
and pines of Acadia National Park.

Above A survey party marching into the
Yellowstone in 1871, the year after Henry
Washburn's expedition opened the campaign to
save Yellowstone. This was to become the first of
America's national parks, in 1872.

Left July evening in Great Sand Dunes
National Park, Colorado. The trees are pinyon
pines, the mountains behind are the Rockies.

Right The ruined "White House" in its
awesome surroundings in Canyon de Chelly
National Monument, Arizona.

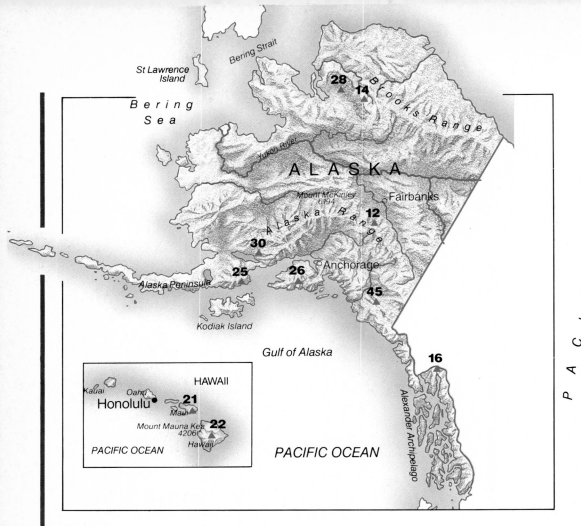

NATIONAL PARKS OF AMERICA

1 ACADIA NATIONAL PARK, PO Box 177, Bar Harbor, ME 04609

2 ARCHES NATIONAL PARK, 446 S.Main St, Moab, UT 84532

3 BADLANDS NATIONAL PARK, PO Box 6, Interior, SD 57750

4 BIG BEND NATIONAL PARK, Big Bend National Park, TX 79834

5 BISCAYNE NATIONAL PARK, PO Box 1369, Homestead, FL 33030

6 BRYCE CANYON NATIONAL PARK, Bryce Canyon, UT 84717

7 CANYONLANDS NATIONAL PARK, 446 S.Main St, Moab, UT 84532

8 CAPITOL REEF NATIONAL PARK, Torrey, UT 84775

9 CARLSBAD CAVERNS NATIONAL PARK, 3225 National Parks Hwy, Carlsbad, NM 88220

10 CHANNEL ISLANDS NATIONAL PARK, 1901 Spinnaker Dr., Ventura, CA 93001

11 CRATER LAKE NATIONAL PARK, PO Box 7, Crater Lake, OR 97604

12 DENALI NATIONAL PARK AND PRESERVE, PO Box 9, Denali, AK 99755

13 EVERGLADES NATIONAL PARK, PO Box 279, Homestead, FL 33030

14 GATES OF THE ARCTIC NATIONAL PARK AND PRESERVE, PO Box 74680, Fairbanks, AK 99707

15 GLACIER NATIONAL PARK, West Glacier, MT 59936

16 GLACIER BAY NATIONAL PARK AND PRESERVE, Gustavus, AK 99826

17 GRAND CANYON NATIONAL PARK, PO Box 129, Grand Canyon, AZ 86023

18 GRAND TETON NATIONAL PARK, PO Drawer 170, Moose, WY 83012

19 GREAT SMOKY MOUNTAINS NATIONAL PARK, Gatlinburg, TN 37738

20 GUADALUPE MOUNTAINS NATIONAL PARK, 3225 National Parks Hwy, Carlsbad, NM 88220

21 HALEAKALA NATIONAL PARK, PO Box 369, Makawao, Maui, HI 96768

22 HAWAII VOLCANOES NATIONAL PARK, Hawaii National Park, HI 96718

23 HOT SPRINGS NATIONAL PARK, PO Box 1860, Hot Springs National Park, AR 71901

24 ISLE ROYALE NATIONAL PARK, 87 N. Ripley St, Houghton, MI 49931

25 KATMAI NATIONAL PARK AND PRESERVE, PO Box 7, King Salmon, AK 99613

26 KENAI FJORDS NATIONAL PARK, PO Box 1727, Seward, AK 99664

27 KINGS CANYON NATIONAL PARK, Three Rivers, CA 93271

28 KOBUK VALLEY NATIONAL PARK, PO Box 287, Kotzebue, AK 99752

29 LASSEN VOLCANIC NATIONAL PARK, Mineral, CA 96063

30 LAKE CLARK NATIONAL PARK AND PRESERVE, 701 C St, PO Box 61, Anchorage, AK 99513

31 MAMMOTH CAVE NATIONAL PARK, Mammoth Cave, KY 42259

32 MESA VERDE NATIONAL PARK, Mesa Verde National Park, CO 81330

33 MOUNT RAINIER NATIONAL PARK, Tahoma Woods, Star Route, Ashford, WA 98304

34 NORTH CASCADES NATIONAL PARK, 800 State St, Sedro Woolley, WA 98284

35 OLYMPIC NATIONAL PARK, 600 E. Park Ave, Port Angeles, WA 98362

36 PETRIFIED FOREST NATIONAL PARK, PO Box 217, Petrified Forest, AZ 86028

37 REDWOOD NATIONAL PARK, 1111 2nd St, Crescent City, CA 95531

38 ROCKY MOUNTAIN NATIONAL PARK, Estes Park, CO 80517

39 SEQUOIA NATIONAL PARK, Three Rivers, CA 93271

40 SHENANDOAH NATIONAL PARK, Luray, VA 22835

41 THEODORE ROOSEVELT NATIONAL PARK, PO Box 7, Medora, ND 58645

42 VIRGIN ISLANDS NATIONAL PARK, PO Box 7789, St Thomas, VI 00801

43 VOYAGEURS NATIONAL PARK, PO Box 50, International Falls, MN 56649

44 WIND CAVE NATIONAL PARK, Hot Springs, SD 57747

45 WRANGELL-ST ELIAS NATIONAL PARK AND PRESERVE, PO Box 29, Glennallen, AK 99588

46 YELLOWSTONE NATIONAL PARK, PO Box 168, Yellowstone National Park, WY 82190

47 YOSEMITE NATIONAL PARK, PO Box 577, Yosemite National Park, CA 95389

48 ZION NATIONAL PARK, Springdale, UT 84767

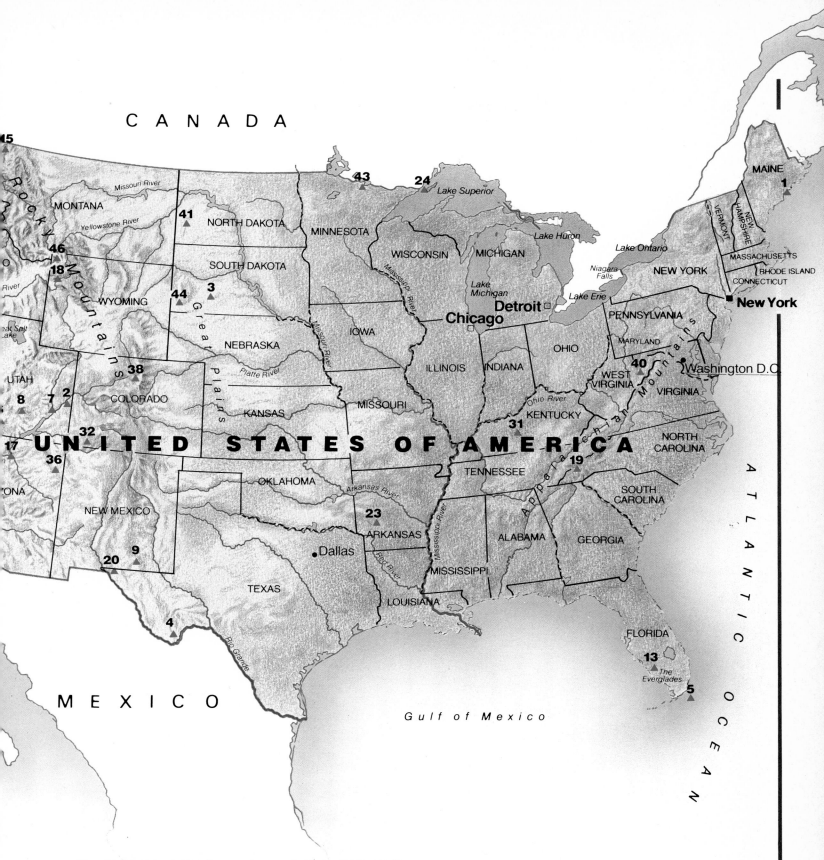

OTHER NATIONAL PARK SITES

ASSATEAGUE ISLAND NATIONAL SEASHORE, Rt 2, Box 294, Berlin, MD 21782

CABRILLO NATIONAL MONUMENT, PO Box 6670, San Diego, CA 92106

CAPE COD NATIONAL SEASHORE, South Wellfleet, MA 02663

CAPE HATTERAS NATIONAL SEASHORE, Rt 1, Box 675, Manteo, NC 27954

FIRE ISLAND NATIONAL SEASHORE, 120 Laurel St, Patchogue, NY 11772

GULF ISLANDS NATIONAL SEASHORE (Florida Unit), PO Box 100, Gulf Breeze, FL 32561

GULF ISLANDS NATIONAL SEASHORE (Mississippi Unit), 3500 Park Rd, Ocean Springs, MS 39564

PADRE ISLAND NATIONAL SEASHORE, 9405 S. Padre Island Dr., Corpus Christi, TX 78418

On June 30, 1864, the United States Congress passed an act granting the Yosemite Valley to the State of California "upon the express conditions that the premises shall be held for public use, resort and recreation." Such a grant of land was without precedent, unknown in the affairs of governments the world over. Scenic and hunting preserves had been the prerogative of royalty, but nowhere had land ever been set aside for all the people.

Once done, it must have been a good idea, for eight years later on March 1, 1872, the first truly national park, Yellowstone, was established "as a public park or pleasuring-ground for the benefit and enjoyment of the people." Immediately tourists from all corners of the country, and the world, began coming to Yellowstone. By 1890, three more national parks were created, and Yosemite was one of them.

Today there are more than 330 areas in the National Park System. They range in size from the new Wrangell-St. Elias National Park in Alaska, the largest with more than eight million acres, to Thaddeus Kosciuszko National Memorial in Philadelphia, one of the smallest. And the system continues to grow. What began quietly without much fanfare in the midst of the tumultuous Civil War years has developed into the world's largest collection of parklands "for the people." And every one of them is a national treasure. Every one in its own way is a "scenic wonder."

This books touches on only a few of the greatest of the scenic wonders of our National Parks — Arches, Glacier, Yosemite, Hawaii Volcanoes, Grand Canyon, Great Smoky Mountains. Some day, each of these will find its way into the language of the twenty-first century as "wonders of the world."

Above right   Early morning at the dream-like beach of Point Reyes, California.

Below right   A Hawaiian volcano erupting: a magnificent red-hot fountain shoots high into the sky. The lava will fall as hot cinders or glassy, wind-formed fragments.

Below   Passive majesty of the giant sculptures at Mount Rushmore.

Above left *Vegetation chokes the water in this everglades swamp, Florida.*

Below left *The intense blue of a mountain lake in the North Cascade range, California. This valley's shape is typical of the starting point of an ancient, long since melted glacier.*

Right *Spring flowers in the North Cascades.*

Below *Sunlit snows on Mount McKinley, Denali National Park and Preserve, Alaska.*

Main picture *Leaves turn flame-colored in October in the Sierra Nevadas.*

Inset *Here the leaves are a brilliant yellow.*

Right Arizona's Petrified Forest: a fossil tree that fell long ago, in the distant Triassic period. Erosion in recent times has exposed the trunk after millions of years underground.

Below Close-up of a piece of petrified wood.

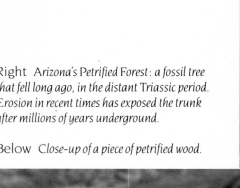

1

NATURE'S ARTISTRY

Arches National Park, high above the Colorado River canyon in southeastern Utah, contains the largest known concentration of natural stone arches in the world, in a landscape at once so beautiful and so startling that one can only stand breathless in awe of nature's way with the building of the earth. This is the Colorado Plateau, that huge red-rock region that lies between the Rocky Mountains and the great Nevada basin, where the Colorado and Green rivers meet in a fantasy world of sculptured rock. This is Canyonland country. Canyonlands National Park is next door; the Grand Canyon is 200 miles down the Colorado; and off in the southwestern corner of the state are Bryce Canyon and Zion National Parks.

There is nothing in the world quite like the geological formations found at Arches — some 200 sandstone rock arches, cut by wind and water in a continuing process that goes on almost before the eyes. That is, there were more than 200 arches at the latest count; there are remote areas of the park in which no one has yet set foot, and any count is only as good as nature may have provided for that day. The landscape will be changed tomorrow. Until the fall of 1940, Skyline Arch was known as Arch-in-the-Making; more than half of its opening was filled with a large fractured, sandstone block. Then one night in November, something dramatic happened. No one saw it; no one heard it. The block crumbled and doubled the arch's span to its present 69 feet. And that, say the rangers, is how it is done.

Or probably that is how it is done ... probably because even though these things happen almost under our noses, we still don't *see* the process. Water froze in the fractures of the block, finally expanding them to their limit. Probably water dissolved the fine cement-like fit of sand grains and probably the wind-carried loose sand wore away at this corner or that until ... the arch was formed.

What happened in this strange but beautiful land in Utah stretches the imagination beyond its limits. Even when the most articulate of geologists talks about shallow seas, giant oceans, millions of years of sedimentary deposits, the lifting of whole sections of the earth...it staggers the mind. There is nothing with which to compare such upheavals. Early explorers thought the huge arches and monoliths were, like Stonehenge in England and the statues of Easter Island, the work of lost cultures, and but for our sophisticated acceptance of scientific theories, we too would suspect the handiwork of some human intelligence.

Above Double Arch in the Arches National Park. Some of the strata are vertical, showing that earth movement has pushed these rocks up on end.

Right An aerial view of Canyon de Chelly, Arizona. Rising from the canyon floor almost to the height of the surrounding plateau is the striking pinnacle of Spider Rock.

Previous pages Landscape Arch in the Arches National Park — the second widest natural arch in the US.

Arches National Park, indeed this whole section of Utah, lies atop a vast underground salt bed, thousands of yards thick in places, that was deposited over the Colorado Plateau 300 million years ago when an ocean covered the land. The ocean then evaporated, and for eons after that, the remaining salt bed was covered with deposits from floods and winds and other seas that came and went. The deposit thus formed is perhaps as much as one mile thick, a subtle blend of densities and textures known today as Entrada Sandstone.

Salt is unstable, so the great salt bed beneath was no match for the enormous weight of the immense layer of rock on top. Under pressure, the salt bed shifted, buckled, liquified, and repositioned itself, thrusting the earth layers upward into domes. Sections dropped into cavities. Faults opened. Hugh rock sections were turned on edge. As the earth was shaped by this sub-surface movement, surface erosion began to take its toll, stripping the younger layers of sandstone. Then, as happened with Arch-in-the-Making, water frozen in cracks, wind-carried sand, and extremes of heat and cold imperceptibly whittled away the weakest layers until only the firmly cemented arches were left.

The smallest arch in the park has an opening 3 feet wide. Landscape Arch is the largest; it measures 105 feet across the narrowest part of its ribbon-like height, and 291 feet from base to base. Until 1983, Landscape Arch was believed to be the largest natural arch in the world. That summer, geologists with laser-beam measuring equipment discovered that Kolob Arch at Zion National Park was 310 feet.

Right *Druid Arch in Canyonlands. It might have reminded early pioneers of England's Stonehenge, but it is purely the work of natural forces.*

Below *Fisheye Arch in Canyonlands.*

Above *Delicate Arch: all that is left where once a rock wall stood. Eventually the leg on the left will fall, and the arch will collapse.*

Left *Sunset at Arches National Park, with Delicate Arch in the background.*

Delicate Arch, probably the most popular in the park, rises gracefully 65 feet into the air along the edge of a deep sandstone bowl, slowly carved from what once was a massive rock wall. Its opening is 35 feet wide and there is a narrow, worn place on one of its legs. Some day, perhaps in the presence of witnesses, Delicate Arch, like so many before it, will crumble, its weakened leg finally worn through. Its loss will be mourned by geologists, but other delicate arches will slowly form, and this great garden of natural sculptures will continue to grow.

Natural arches, formed by wind, extreme temperatures, and pressures, should not be confused with natural *bridges*, formed by the erosive action of running water. Natural bridges — three of which were found in southern Utah in 1883, with the most spectacular, Rainbow Bridge, being found in 1909—are *enlarged* and *shaped* by the same forces that begin arches, but *bridges* always begin through the action of stream or river erosion. Owachomo, Sipapu, and Kachina bridges are in Natural Bridges National Monument; Rainbow Bridge is a national monument by itself.

The rock at Natural Bridges is a sandstone similar to that found at Arches, vulnerable to any form of erosion. Here at White and Armstrong canyons, the relentless flow of streams scouring long winding curves, some looping into tight S formations, has scraped away at thin walls of sandstone until a break has finally occurred. Eventually the water breaks through to take the shortest course through the opening, thus creating the arch or bridge. Time and other natural erosive forces have created huge openings until today we have arches that are bridges. Kachina and Sipapu bridges still straddle winding streams, and floodwaters continue to work away at their sides. The stream beneath Owachomo Bridge no longer runs, but the bridge itself is in danger. Its span is 180 feet and its width at the highest point is 27 feet, but its thickness is only 9 feet and it may have a fatal crack. While it is not likely that this generation will see it fall, of the three bridges, Owachomo is the one that will yield to erosion soonest.

Left   The wind and the weather were the sculptors and architects that created Sunset Point, Bryce Canyon National Park, Utah.

Below   Close-up showing just a few of Bryce Canyon's astonishing cathedral-like spires.

Rainbow Bridge. *Nonnezoshi*, the Navajos called it, meaning "rainbow of stone." This is the most spectacular of all natural bridges, rising 290 feet above Bridge Canyon, and spanning 275 feet. It was first discovered by the white man in 1909 when a survey party set out with the express purpose of locating the legendary sacred Navajo stone arch. The top is 33 feet wide and 42 feet thick at its thinnest point. This natural wonder nestles among a myriad of canyons carved by streams flowing to the Colorado River from the north flank of Navajo Mountain. Until lake Powell filled Glenn Canyon and backed up Bridge Creek to the bridge itself, Rainbow Bridge was in one of the most inaccessible regions of the contiguous United States.

The base of Rainbow Bridge is composed of Kayenta Formation, reddish-brown to purplish consolidations of sands and muds laid down hundreds of millions of years ago. Above its base the bridge is composed of Navajo Sandstone. This formation was created as wave upon wave of sand dunes were deposited to depths of 1,000 feet. Over the next 100 million years, both of these formations were buried more than 5,000 feet deep by still other strata of sediments. Extreme pressures and temperatures consolidated and hardened the rock of these formations.

Above right Fossilized dinosaur bones, discovered in the Colorado Rockies.

Below right Erosion has worn away the weaker parts of a sandstone plateau, leaving this complicated shape.

Below The North Window in Arches National Park. Its name recalls cathedral architecture, as do the spires of Bryce Canyon.

Some 60 million years ago the Colorado Plateau began a gradual uplift. Today's landscape results from the erosion caused by streams cutting into these massive layers of rock now lifted far above sea level. As the landscape lifted and tilted, these streams acquired more force and began to carve and cut through the rock.

As Bridge Creek entrenched itself into the landscape, the scene was set for carving Rainbow Bridge. As the waters cut through the Navajo Sandstone and then hit the hard Kayenta Formation rock, the cutting became more difficult. The stream then widened its path and undercut the canyon walls. Finally it cut through the neck of a meander loop. The stream then altered its course, taking the more direct route through the break. Huge flakes of sandstone broke loose and fell, leaving a conchoidal or shell-like pattern similar to that found in the chipping of Indian arrowheads. Natural flaking, called exfoliation, contributes to the formation of alcoves and natural bridges throughout this region.

Rainbow Bridge was recognized in 1910 as a national monument. Today the 160,000 acres of land around the bridge adjoining Lake Powell constitute one of the true jewels in the National Park System. And no longer is it so isolated. It still belongs to the great stone wilderness of the Colorado Plateau, but it is accessible by car, and by boat on Lake Powell.

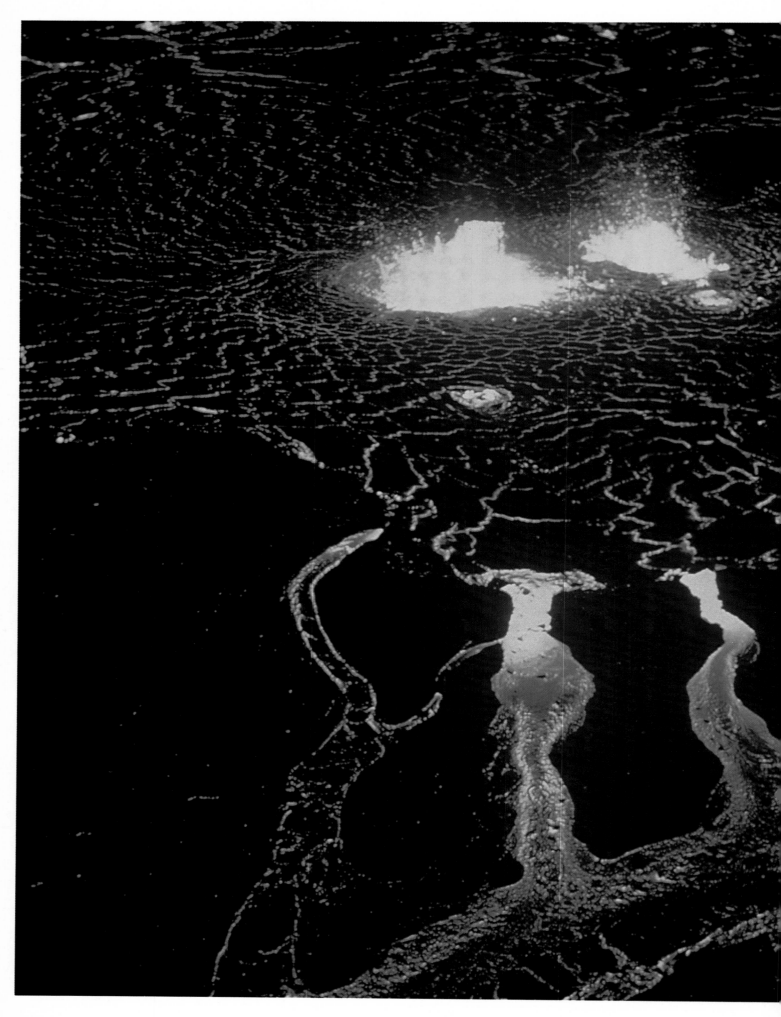

2

FROM THE CENTER OF THE EARTH

The Hawaii Natural History Association at Hawaii Volcanoes National Park, in co-operation with the National Park Service, produced a video tape on the eruption of Hawaii's Mauna Loa Volcano called "Rivers of Fire." It is available to the public, and is, without doubt, one of the most exciting nature films ever made. The following brief description of the 1984 eruption paraphrases a portion of the film's narration.

Mauna Loa, the world's largest shield volcano, awakens after a restless repose of nine years. It is March 25, 1984. For the next 21 days a pent-up power in the earth drives more than two hundred million cubic yards of magma from an internal sea, a mass sufficient to pave a highway to the moon.

This Sunday morning the eruption begins near the volcano's summit of 13,677 feet ... fissures later open at 11,200 feet and at 9,400 feet. The lava forms channels like rivers of water. Within the first 24 hours, the main flow advances eight miles down the northeast flank. The river swells to depths of 15 feet at temperatures of 2,100°F. It descends to an elevation of 6,200 feet.

First there is the eruption of the summit caldera, a red ribbon placed on edge, a curtain of fire as high as the Statue of Liberty, as long as New York's Central Park. Eight hours later, another major episode, as a vent outbreak occurs farther down the mountain at 11,200 feet; another seven hours later, a vent outbreak again, this time at 9,400 feet. This latest vent will be the principal source of lava for the next 20 days — the main tap. Every hour, nearly a million cubic yards of magma flows from the deep unseen hotspots ... enough mass every 60 minutes to fill an area the size of Disneyland to a depth of nearly 10 feet.

Day five ... molten lava twists down its channels, red hot coals on a conveyor belt. Molten rivers overflow their channels to become ponds. The rivers now slither a distance of 16 miles and descend to an elevation of 3,200 feet.

Day six ... now 25 miles to the east, Kilauea, more restless than Mauna Loa, erupts ... it has erupted more than sixty times since the early 1800s. For the first time in 65 years, two of Hawaii's volcanoes are erupting simultaneously ...

The pictures are brilliant with color, the devastation to the landscape is complete, the power and force from within the earth is awesome. Hawaii, through its volcanoes, is once again rebuilding itself or, more accurately, it is continuing the construction of the chain of Pacific mountains of which it is part.

As these words are being written, Mauna Loa is threatening to erupt again, as is Mount St. Helens. It has been just five years since the top of this seemingly quiescent mountain in the state of Washington thundered into the atmosphere, and showed us that all is not calm beneath the surface of the earth. The Pacific "Ring of Fire" is misbehaving and in this generation we may see more massive explosions at these and other volcanic sites around the Pacific circle.

The Hawaiian chain of Pacific islands offers a new piece to the puzzle almost every day. Here the earth continues to shift, change, reshape itself, reveal its past. Hawaii is a living laboratory, one of the few places in the world where the lay person can sit side-by-side with the scientist, virtually on the edge of a volcano, and watch the constant process of building and reshaping.

Hawaii, the largest of the eight major islands in the Hawaiian Islands, is almost hypnotic in its serenity and beauty, but its lush vegetation, beautiful waterfalls and shorelines, and unpolluted atmosphere all belie the incredible energy simmering beneath.

Unlike the Grand Canyon and Arches and Zion, where erosion is measured in hundreds of years, the island of Hawaii grows almost on an hourly basis. The most recent eruption from Mauna Loa and Kilauea added millions of cubic yards of new lava, the stuff from which these islands are made, in just a matter of days. The process is as startling as the scientific explanation behind it.

Left As a stream of running lava cools, it first forms a skin which gets folded and twisted by the action of the still flowing lava underneath. The result is a "ropy lava" known as pahoehoe.

Below The rocky coast of Kauai, the next island towards the west from Honolulu, Hawaii.

Right The vast interior of Haleakala Crater on the island of Maui, Hawaii. From the crater floor rise smaller cones, the products of more recent eruptions.

Below Trees killed by a cinder fall from a fiery fountain eruption, Hawaii.

Left Down by the coast on Kauai lies the unique and beautiful fern forest of Kilauea.

Right The knife-like Koolau mountain range runs along the east shore of the island of Oahu, Hawaii.

Below Fern grotto on Kauai, where ferns have begun to colonize the bare volcanic rock.

Left *Waimea Canyon on Kauai, as seen from the specially constructed visitors' viewpoint.*

Below *Piimonga Falls offer a refreshing break from Hawaii's tropical heat.*

The Hawaiian Islands are just one of the best examples of "plate tectonics" on the globe. The earth's crust is made up of a number of sections or plates that move about as though gliding over a fluid mantle beneath. The Pacific plate is one of these and the Hawaiian Islands are right in the middle of it. The plate is moving, imperceptibly, towards the northwest and taking the islands with it. Somewhere beneath all of this is a "hot spot," a vent through which molten lava is forced to the earth's surface by internal pressures of incredible magnitude. At one time the mountains and islands to the northwest were directly over this vent — Kohala at the northwest end of the island of Hawaii, Haleakala on Maui — but now Mauna Loa and Kilauea are directly over it and we can literally see the progression of volcanic life and death.

Each of these islands, when over the hot spot, was formed of the lava forced to the surface. As the plate moved on, at a rate of between 3 and 5 inches a year, the volcanoes were severed from their earth-building source and died. Life erupted again, over the same vent in the mantle, a few million years later and a few miles to the southeast. At this rate, in 12,672 years from now, it is estimated, Hawaii will be one mile to the northwest. In three to five million years from now it will be about where Honolulu is today, and ... far into the future, some seventy million years from now, Hawaii will reach the edge of the Pacific plate near where the Aleutian Islands are today, where it will meet the Asian plate and be folded back into the mantle from which it came. Time scales and distances too large to comprehend ... When all this comes to pass, new paradises will have risen from the floor of the Pacific, and the earth's evolution will go on as before.

Hawaii Volcanoes National Park is one of the great wonders of the world, and certainly one of the most exciting parks in the system. Its beauty is beyond compare; its scientific significance is inestimable.

Above Birds of Hawaii include the masked booby, a fish-eater related to the gannet.

Left (main picture) Iao Needle, Hawaii: a silent monument to some cataclysmic eruption, long ago.

Inset Hawaii has a unique assortment of native plants. This one is Vaccinium reticulatum, with its attractive berries.

Left Calm of the Pacific; a magical sunset at Hawaii. From here it's nothing but ocean, scattered islands, and more ocean, all the way to China and Japan.

Below Coconut palms and a beach of black sand at Hiamu, Hawaii.

3

AFTER THE GLACIERS RETREATED

Nestled among the glacier-sculptured Sierra Nevada is Yosemite National Park, the closest place to paradise anywhere on earth. The great American naturalist John Muir recognized as much: "Things frail and fleeting ... meet and blend in countless forms, as if into this one mountain mansion Nature had gathered her choicest treasures."

The Sierra Nevada is not a series of mountains, like the Rockies or Cascades, but rather a single block of solid granite extending 400 miles north and south near California's eastern border and ranging from 50 to 80 miles wide. It is the longest and highest unbroken mountain range in the lower 48 states, thrust up and then tilted by unimaginable geological forces deep within the earth. The Sierra rises from low foothills on the western side to 14,000 feet and then drops off precipitously on the eastern side.

"The Incomparable Valley," as Yosemite has been called, is probably the world's best known example of a glacier-carved canyon. During the formation of the Sierra range, when sedimentary layers left by the shallow edges of the Pacific Ocean eroded and the granite was exposed and tilted, streams and rivers, like the Merced, rapidly cut deep V-shaped valleys. Snows in the higher elevations compacted into glaciers that further broadened the valleys, canyons, and basins, and left in their wake an ancient lake, the bed of which is now the Yosemite Valley floor. Standing guard over this mile-long, Eden-like landscape are giant granite spires, domes and monoliths, "so compactly and harmoniously arranged," John Muir wrote, "that the valley ... looks like an immense hall or temple lighted from above." Two of these, El Capitan, the world's largest solid granite rock, and Half Dome, dominate at either end of the valley.

Yosemite Valley is a mosaic of open meadows sprinkled with wild flowers and flowering shrubs, oak woodlands, and mixed-conifer forests of ponderosa pine, incense cedar and Douglas fir. Wildlife, from monarch butterflies to mule deer and black bears, flourishes in these communities. Around the valley's perimeter, waterfalls, which reach their maximum flow in May and June, crash to the floor. Yosemite has more than half of America's highest waterfalls. In the spring, when the high snows melt, streams that once flowed continuously into rivers, their channels now cut away, leap into the open air and create some of the most beautiful sights in the valley. Yosemite Falls drop 2,425 feet, more than thirteen times as high as the mighty Niagara Falls.

But Yosemite Valley is only a small percentage of this large national park of some 1,180 square miles. The Tuolumne Meadows and high country of Yosemite have some of the most rugged, sublime scenery in the Sierra. In the summer the meadows, lakes, and exposed granite slopes teem with life. Due to the short growing season, the plants and animals here take maximum advantage of the warm days to grow, bloom, and store food for the long, cold winter.

The Tioga Road (California Route 120), originally built as a mining road in 1882-3 was realigned and modernized in 1961 as a scenic highway and now crosses this area. The road passes through an area of sparkling lakes, meadows, domes, and lofty peaks that only 10,000 years ago lay under glacier ice. Scenic turnouts all along the road afford superb views. At Tioga Pass the road crosses the Sierra's crest at 9,945 feet, the highest automobile pass in California. Here you see two striking contrasts: to the west, peaks and meadows; to the east, high desert.

Tuolumne Meadows, at 8,600 feet above sea level, is the largest subalpine meadow in the Sierra. It is 55 miles from Yosemite Valley via the Tioga Road. Long a focal point of summer activity, it is now growing in popularity as a winter mountaineering area. In the summer Tuolumne Meadows is a favorite starting point for backpacking trips and day hikes. The meadows are spectacular in early summer, abounding in wild flowers and wildlife.

Above Black bear, an inhabitant of Yosemite, investigating an old log.

Left Yosemite Falls: the Upper Fall plunges 1,430 feet over the Valley's north wall; the Lower Fall just below is a drop of over 300 feet. Combined with the cascades in between, the falls' double leap measures 2,425 feet.

Far left Wild flowers in a meadow on the floor of the Yosemite Valley.

Previous pages Near the entrance to the Yosemite Valley, the looming crag of El Capitan rises 3,604 feet above the valley floor.

49

Glacier Point is one of those rare places where the scenery is so vast that it overwhelms the viewer. Just below a sheer rock cliff, about 3,200 feet straight down, one gets a bird's-eye view of the length and breadth of Yosemite Valley. Across the valley one can see the entire 2,425-foot drop of Yosemite Falls. And beyond, the panoramic expanse of the High Sierra stands out in awe-inspiring clarity. Sunset and full-moon nights are ideal times to visit the point. During full-moon, millions of stars overhead and the pastel granites of the landscape change into something surrealistic. In the summer one can drive to Glacier Point — it is just 32 miles from the valley; in winter, when the road is closed at Summit Meadow, Glacier Point is a favorite rendezvous for cross-country skiers. But no matter how you arrive or when you go, Glacier Point offers Yosemite's finest view.

Another outstanding feature of Yosemite National Park is the giant Sequoia tree. The Mariposa Grove, 35 miles south of the valley, is the largest of three Sequoia groves in the park. The Tuolumne and Merced Groves are near Crane Flat. Despite political pressures, these towering giants, largest of all living things, have endured for thousands of years, perhaps since the beginning of history of the Western world. The Mariposa Grove's Grizzly Giant is 2,700 years old and is thought to be the oldest of all Sequoias.

Above Besides the mighty Yosemite Falls, the National Park has five other waterfalls: Ribbon, Bridal Veil, Vernal, Illilouette and (shown here) Nevada Falls.

Right The massive red trunk of a Sequoia in Yosemite, which has split at the base and has been treated with a preservative: it could live for a few more centuries yet.

Wawona, an Indian word meaning "big tree", was the site of a wayside hostel built in 1857 by Galen Clark, the first guardian of the Yosemite Grant. Known as Clark's Station, it served as an overnight stop for visitors in transit between Yosemite Valley and Mariposa. In 1857, the year the original Wawona Road was opened, the Washburn brothers purchased the area and built the Wawona Hotel, still in operation today. This is the setting of the Pioneer Yosemite History Center, a collection of furnished and relocated historic buildings and historic horse-drawn coaches.

Yosemite is one of America's great treasures. Its wilderness (over 1,500 kinds of trees and plants), its wildlife (some 80 species of animals and more than 200 species of birds), and its incredible beauty are things that can never be forgotten once seen. Upon entering the valley in 1850, Major James D. Savage, one of the early soldier-settlers, said: "It looks to me just as I suspected it would look. It's a hell of a place!"

Gold was never found in Yosemite. Instead we found a treasure more rare and beautiful — cliffs so high and granite mountains so huge they staggered even the most hardened explorers; giant Sequoia trees so old they defied any known means of measuring time; waterfalls that came from the sky and plunged into eternity; and a wilderness so vast and remote that to this day no one has seen it all. Yosemite was and is Nature at its greatest intensity and loving tenderness. It must be kept that way.

John Muir wrote: "These sacred mountain temples are the holiest ground that the heart of man has consecrated, and it behooves us all faithfully to do our part in seeing that our wild mountain parks are passed on unspoiled to those who come after us, for they are national properties to which every man has right and interest."

John Muir was a prophet; Yosemite has been his beacon. Those who pass through the Valley and read his words will never forget.

Above *The upper end of Yosemite Valley broadens with a semicircle of granite domes: Sentinel Basket, North Dome and (shown) the massive Half Dome.*

Above left *The lower end of Yosemite Valley. Silt, sand and rock filled the glacial lake that once lay here, creating the present strikingly level valley floor.*

Left *El Capitan in winter: Yosemite is as enchanting and imposing in winter as in summer.*

The great ice ages began three million years ago. There were four of them, in fact, and they spread across North America molding the landscape as we know it. The last, the Wisconsin Ice Age, was responsible for what we see at Glacier National Park in the United States and Waterton National Park across the border in Canada. All of this came about, of course, after the proverbial "great shallow sea" had left its many layers of sediment across Northwest America one billion years ago, and after the uplifts and folds of the mountains formed 75 million years ago.

The largest of these great upheavals of the earth's crust was the Rocky Mountain chain, which extends from Mexico, through the continental United States, Canada, and Alaska, and on to the Aleutians. But nowhere in this chain is the mountain wilderness quite as majestic as at Glacier National Park and its sister park across the border. "Give a month at least to this precious reserve," wrote John Muir. "The time will not be taken from the sum of your life. Instead of shortening, it will indefinitely lengthen it and make you truly immortal."

Glacier is a place where the process of layering is very obvious, where

Below Glacier's Two Medicine Lake (on the Two Medicine River) is a natural for camping, boating and hiking; it also offers excellent fishing.

over millions of years the various sediments were compressed and cemented into rock strata we now identify by their color — red, green, gray, and buff. During the mountain-building age, which lasted for millions of years, tremendous pressures beneath the earth's crust uplifted and folded over these layers of sedimentary rock. Concentrated into a comprehensible time frame, as if by stop-action photography, the monstrous forces that produced this buckling and cracking would be cataclysmic. Huge rock layers were stood on end, others crumbled, still others were thrust upward and over their neighbors so that in time young rock overlaid old. Unlike the Southern or Colorado Rockies, this 300-mile range was squeezed together in a vise-like grip that forced the rock sideways to the east in a fold called an overthrust. The geological formations that comprise Glacier's east wall show that this mass was pushed some 40 miles eastward. Approached from the east, these mountains offer the impression that they were pushed up right there. There are no foothills as there are on the western slope. The farthest extension of this overthrust is Chief Mountain in the northeast corner of the park.

After all of this had taken place, the great ice ages pushed their glaciers down from the north, sculpting the valleys and canyons and slicing and rounding the mountains. There are more than fifty glaciers in the park today, some of which formed 4,000 years ago, others only 1,000 years ago. But still they carve and cut and shape the landscape, although perhaps not as fast as those ice giants that preceded them. But they are rapidly melting away.

At the height of the glacial periods, these valleys were filled with ice as much as 3,000 feet thick, and at least one glacier extended 40 miles into the Montana plains. The paths of these glaciers can be measured by the knife-like ridges, the peaks, the passes, the valleys, and in particular by the debris they left behind. Some flowed quite rapidly — rapidly for a glacier — attaining a speed of several feet a day. Today's glaciers flow more slowly. Grinnell, for example, has been "clocked" at about one inch a day. Nonetheless, it is the constant motion of the thick, plastic-like ice at the bottom of glaciers, combined with the huge boulders and rocks imbedded in them, that slices through mountains and digs valleys and basins.

Glacier National Park is the only area south of the Canadian border that has a subarctic climate, and the plant and animal life reflect this. Despite the deceptively barren appearance of the mountains, the park is a sanctuary for a wide variety of wildlife and plants. The western slopes capture the abundant rainfall from the Pacific coast and are clothed in dense forests of larch, spruce, fir, and lodgepole pine. Here the western red cedar and hemlock reach their eastern boundaries. On the east side, where the Montana plains and the mountains abruptly meet, the prairie flora prevails: pasque flowers, red and white geraniums, gaillardia, asters, shooting stars, and the Indian paintbrush plant. The short-lived alpine display is every bit as splendid and can be easily seen along the hundreds of miles of trails through the upper reaches of the park.

Left *Beargrass in bloom along a creek in Glacier National Park, with mountain mist aloft.*

Below *The Indian paintbrush plant in full bloom, its splayed petals showing their orangey-red tips.*

Bottom *A cow moose with her calves in Glacier National Park.*

One of the joys of Glacier National Park is that the wildlife, once hunted for sport and food, is now protected. Deer, elk, moose, and bear are abundant and for the most part easily seen by the visitor. We humans confer the label "official" on many things: here we have given this distinction to the mountain goat, the "official" animal of Glacier National Park. This nimble mammal wears its title unpretentiously. Actually it is an antelope and not a goat at all, but seen scampering along the most precipitous cliffs and precarious rock formations, titles and names matter little to it or the visitor. It is a marvelous animal that astounds you and at the same time makes you envious of its agility.

Peter Fidler, a scout for the Hudson's Bay Company in 1792, was the first white man to see the Wateron-Glacier area. He found the Piggan Indians had been there long before and, no doubt, other prehistoric Indian communities prior to that. Settlement was slow and tedious through the nineteenth century, made difficult by rugged terrain and fierce Indian reluctance to yield up territory. The conquering of the Indians came about much as it did in other areas of the West; ultimately economic factors — the pressures of the fur trade and mining interests — forced a withdrawal and settlers from the East moved in.

The Great Northern Railroad was as responsible as anything for the development of Glacier National Park. By 1891 there was a line across Montana and over Marias Pass to Kalispell, along the southern end of the area. Thirty years after the railroad came, mining potential decreased dramatically. The Great Northern, politicians, and conservationists then joined hands in urging Congress to preserve the area in its natural state. Glacier became a national park on May 11, 1910.

Nowhere is the work of glaciers so dramatically displayed as here in Montana. Glacier has been called the "Crown of the Continent," — justly, for its mountains unfold into a huge diadem of cathedral-like spires.

Left *View from Logan Pass in Glacier, on the way to the 10,014-foot Mount Siyeh.*

Far left *Inhospitable slopes high in the Rockies: a roadside view seen from Gunsight Pass, Glacier National Park.*

4

THE GREAT SMOKY MOUNTAINS

More than 9,000,000 people visit the Great Smoky Mountains National Park every year, a remarkable number considering that there are no great geysers or canyons or jagged snow-covered peaks to climb or admire, no redrock arches or natural bridges to photograph. But the Smokies have their own magic. The Appalachian Mountains of North Carolina and Tennessee, of which they are part, are one of the American nation's greatest treasures.

Of course, one of the reasons for the Smokies' immense popularity is that fact that the park lies within a few hundred miles of the great megalopolis of the eastern seaboard. But beyond that, the Smokies are a "living forest", forever protected from the development and intrusion that once threatened to destroy them. Within the park's 500,000 acres, of which seventy-five percent is wilderness, grow more than 1,400 species of flowering plant. There are 800 miles of trails, 700 miles of streams, and sixteen peaks over 6,000 feet in height. It is possible to hike or, for that matter, drive from great stands of dogwood and redbud trees typical of southern climates, through sugar maples and yellow birches typical of New England, and up to fir and spruce forests typical of Canada all in the space of a day.

This is an ancient land. Some of the first humans to inhabit North America passed through these southern Appalachian Mountains. There is intriguing evidence that some 15,000 years ago nomadic tribes lived here and that their descendants, the Cherokee Indians, one of the largest and most stable of America's early societies, made their homes in the *Shaconage*, "the place of the blue smoke". They hunted and farmed and thrived; but as time went on, they were nearly destroyed, and the land in which they lived was nearly lost.

The Appalachians are the oldest mountains on earth, about 400 million years old, which is about three times older than the Rockies. There was much earth activity before that distant time, and certainly much after it, but geologists agree that this was the main period of mountain-building in the East, a period called the *Appalachian Revolution*. After the oceans had retreated and the earth's crust had finished its great upheavals and the glaciers from the north had completed their carvings, the plants and trees took root. All of this stretches nearly to the last minute of the proverbial scientific timetable. The tragedies of the Smokies came in the very last second of that timetable, between the early 1800s and 1940 when the Great Smoky Mountains National Park was established.

The Appalachian Mountains are not as delicate as the grassland of the Everglades to the south or as tough as the granite peaks of Yosemite to the west, but just as those preserves have been caught in the struggle against the arrogance of man, so have the Great Smokies. Aldo Leopold wrote: "When some remote ancestor of ours invented the shovel, he became a giver; he could plant a tree. And when the axe was invented, he became a taker; he could chop it down." In the Smokies, the axe came first. Sixty-five percent of the primeval forest fell before anyone thought about giving back.

The Cherokee was the first victim. The tribe's first village, Kituwha, was located just inside the present park boundary, near Bryson City, North Carolina, but however advanced their civilization, these people had little defense against the overwhelming tide of English, Scots-Irish, and German settlers who, following the Revolutionary War, pushed through to the fertile lands of the western frontier. By 1828 the Cherokee people had succumbed and, in one of the dark moments of American history, were marched off along the infamous "Trail of Tears" to what is now Oklahoma.

The Indian had not tamed the wilderness; at best it was a compatible relationship where the forest provided the necessities for survival while the Indian left little mark. This was not true of his successor. Within 20 years the valleys and coves had been claimed for settlement, fields had been stripped of ancient rock and trees, and mountain tops were cleared for pasture. A different kind of civilization had arrived. From here on, the Smokies would give. There would be little given in return.

Previous pages Pinetops, long mountain ridges and early morning clouds in the lowlands: the Great Smokies are always full of magical sights like this.

These pages Scenes and sights in the Great Smoky Mountains: (right) violets, lichens and mosses clothe the forest floor; (far right) a wild turkey puts on its "threat" display; (below right) a stream splashes over the stones at Roaring Fork; (below) mixed woodland and mixed colors as fall gets under way.

Life in the Appalachians was isolated, bare of all but the essentials, but that isolation welded several cultures into one. The people of the Appalachians became "the mountain people," surviving in a world of their own making. They were strong, courageous, defiant, tough, and at the same time violent and gentle. Little changed through the years as the world around them evolved; nothing touched them.

Then around the turn of the century the Little River Lumber Company bought 8,600 acres of prime timberland right in the heart of the Smoky Mountains. Land that had not been taken up by farms and grazing was now destined to be brutally harvested. Two-thirds of the forest, trees that had stood for centuries, was cleared to meet the insatiable demands of growing cities all along the eastern seaboard. Streams were dammed and then released to carry logs to mills; railroads were cut through; mill towns sprung up as other lumber companies moved in and the timber industry spread. The mountain people sold their farms and their goods and stood by as first the saw and the axe and then Nature turned the once lush, green country into a scarred, barren wasteland.

The beginnings of Great Smoky Mountains National Park are a story of conflict, confusion, bitterness, politics, the classic confrontation

Above left *Great Smoky Mountains in North Carolina at dawn.*

Above *Craggy Gardens in the Blue Ridge Mountains, North Carolina, with rhododendrons coming into bloom.*

Above right *Great Smoky Mountains at sunset. Amid expansive scenery like this, the people of the mountains live in a separate world from the modern cities of America.*

between conservationist, industry, and homesteader. By 1923 there was still just enough forest left to make it worth the effort to preserve the last virgin forest in the the East, but there were more than 6,000 individually-owned parcels of land in the "park" proposed by private citizens in both North Carolina and Tennessee. It took millions of dollars and many years of emotionally-charged negotiations to weld all of them together, but the park was finally established in 1934.

The mountains today belie this recent and tumultuous history. The forests have come back — there are more than 130 native species of tree — and the wildlife, nearly dissipated by 1934, is now protected and growing. There are about 200 species of bird, 50 species of mammal, 40 reptiles, and 70 fish. And the Cherokee Indians — some of whom hid in the remote areas of the mountains and never really left — have returned from the West to reclaim their original homeland; they live on the Qualla Reservation, once again in the shadow of "the place of the blue smoke."

The Great Smoky Mountains are a microcosm of the geological and human beginnings of the American nation. While most westward expansion was not as violent a conflict between man and wilderness, the Smokies were a test case for future national parks.

5

THE GRAND CANYON OF THE COLORADO RIVER

The great British novelist J.B. Priestley wrote of the Grand Canyon: "Those who have not seen it will not believe any possible description. Those who have seen it know it cannot be described." Preconceived notions vanish; the words of others prove inadequate. This is one place on earth that is indeed beyond description.

The Grand Canyon of the Colorado River defies writers, artists, and photographers alike. All have tried; all have failed. "Though there are elsewhere deep canyons, some of even greater depth than the Grand Canyon," wrote traveler François Matthes, "there is not one that can match its vastness, its majesty, its ornate sculpture and its wealth of color. Whoever stands upon the brink of the Grand Canyon beholds a spectacle unrivaled on this earth."

There is only one way to "see" the Grand Canyon. And only those with vision will *see*. Some have looked but not understood. Exploring the region in 1857, young army lieutenant Joseph Ives wrote: "It seems intended by nature that the Colorado River, along the greater portion of its lonely and majestic way, shall be forever unvisited and undisturbed." It is inconceivable that even in the days before "civilization" had pushed to the very rims of the canyon, anyone could have so totally missed the dazzling beauty spread out before him.

Miraculously, it is possible to see today precisely what Ives saw more than a century ago; I say "miraculously," for the Grand Canyon has survived all sorts of proposed intrusions — a chair-lift to the bottom, bridges of various designs, and dams that would have flooded it. But Ives and his meaningless words have been forgotten, and those who have sought to "enhance" the canyon for future generations have been dismissed, one hopes forever.

This is not a world to be tamed for our pleasure. Unseen forces have created here the most awesome spectacle on earth — a canyon 200 miles long, between 5 and 12 miles wide, and more than a mile deep. The dimensions alone stagger the mind, but even more marvelous are the tremendous forces of nature that built it, and that even to this day continue to shape it. This is the story of the earth itself unfolded before the eye, a geological calendar of time filled with the chaos of creation and the radiance of life going on. No one — not even those without vision — leaves the Grand Canyon unmoved by all this.

When one suddenly comes upon the Grand Canyon — and there is no other way to come upon it except suddenly, such is the nature of the Colorado Plateau — one tends to feel this is *the* discovery. The eye sweeps the great rocks and cliffs and gorges, and the mind drinks in the variety of colors, and then in a matter of seconds it all changes. There are a thousand Grand Canyons as the sun moves across the sky; no view is the same as the one before it. From the brilliance of sunrise and a nearly pure white sky, through the muted reds and golds of sunsets to the soft glow of the moon and stars, the Grand Canyon offers an infinity of moving experiences that mark the soul forever. It is indeed a discovery every time.

Indians have lived along the rims and in the canyon itself for the past 700 years; one tribe, the Havasupai, still farms a small oasis on the canyon floor. It was their ancestors that enticed Spanish explorers into the American Southwest. Lopez de Cardenas and the men of Coronada's expedition saw the canyon in 1540, but they, like Lieutenant Ives, were unimpressed. Searching single-mindedly for legendary Indian cities of gold and silver, the canyon was no more than an inconveniently large natural barrier. It was left to a one-armed Civil War veteran, Major John Wesley Powell, to explore the Colorado River and bring the wonders of the Grand Canyon to the world. Powell's journals are fresh and vibrant and still used as guides along the river.

Ives was wrong too about visitors. In 1880 an ex-miner by the name of John Hance improved the old Indian trails into the canyon from the South Rim and began leading tourists down to the river. By 1901, there were hotels and camps, and within a few years a spur of the Santa Fe Railroad. With these came the entrepreneurs and, fortunately, the conservationists.

Efforts to preserve the canyon as a national park began in 1882, shortly after the establishment of Yellowstone, when Indiana Senator Benjamin Harrison introduced legislation in Congress. One would think that with Yellowstone and Yosemite fresh in the public mind, the

Previous pages *The Grand Canyon in early morning: "Whoever stands upon the brink of the Grand Canyon beholds a spectacle unrivaled on this earth".*

Below *O'Neill Butte in the Grand Canyon, seen at sunset in May from Hopi Point.*

Right *An assortment of cacti and wild flowers on a hillside at Organ Pipe National Monument, Arizona.*

Below *Aspens rising from a small valley in the Navajo National Monument, Arizona; they are just turning yellow as summer ends.*

proposal would have breezed through Washington. Incredible as it may seem, Harrison's bill failed, and it was not until 1893, when he became President, that he was able to protect even the forest around the canyon from mining and timber prospectors. President Theodore Roosevelt established the canyon as a national monument by decree in 1908; 11 years later Grand Canyon National Park was created.

Almost every day geologists learn something new about this planet from their studies in the Grand Canyon. For nearly a century now we have pieced together an astounding story of erosion and upheaval spanning two billion years of geological history. But all we really know for certain is that it is the Colorado River, still flowing and still carving its way to the Pacific Ocean, that has changed this land.

The Colorado begins in the Rocky Mountains and flows 1,450 miles to the Gulf of California. Along the way it is met by dozens of tributaries, the largest of which is the Green River rising from the mountains of Wyoming. The Colorado and its tributaries drain a total land area of 240,000 square miles, dropping 10,000 feet over hundreds of rapids before reaching the sea.

Once, before dams were built in its path, the Colorado ran untamed, carving its way through the canyon at a speed of between 2 and 12 miles an hour. Today its force has been considerably subdued, but still it moves more than a ton of silt every 24 hours, and only when one has grasped this can one imagine what has transpired over the past billions of years.

During the high waters of 1927, more than 27 million tons of suspended solids and dissolved materials were moved in one day. This is to say nothing of the rocks and boulders that were carried across the river bed. Despite these impressive facts, erosion of the river bed and the canyon is exceedingly slow, since scientists have been measuring, about 6½ inches for each 1,000 years.

But it has not been the Colorado alone that has created this massive removal process. There were great land shifts, tiltings caused by pressures from deep in the earth, which caused the river to run faster and erode deeper. As it did so, the canyon sides broke away and crumbled, only to be carried on by the rushing waters. Rain and melting snows caused further erosion, all the time cutting deeper and widening the gap.

And all of this goes on now. Our visits to the Grand Canyon are so short, our time on earth such an infinitesimal moment on the geological time scale, that we are not likely to see any great crumblings or the canyon widening to any significant degree in this generation, but the Colorado will go on grinding and the walls of the canyon will continue to retreat until some day, millions of years from now, only a lazy river will meander across a plain where once we stood.

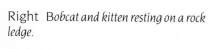
Right Bobcat and kitten resting on a rock ledge.

Far right Looking down into the Grand Canyon from the Kaibab Trail: slowly, rocks continue to flake and crumble into the canyon, imperceptibly widening it as the centuries go by.

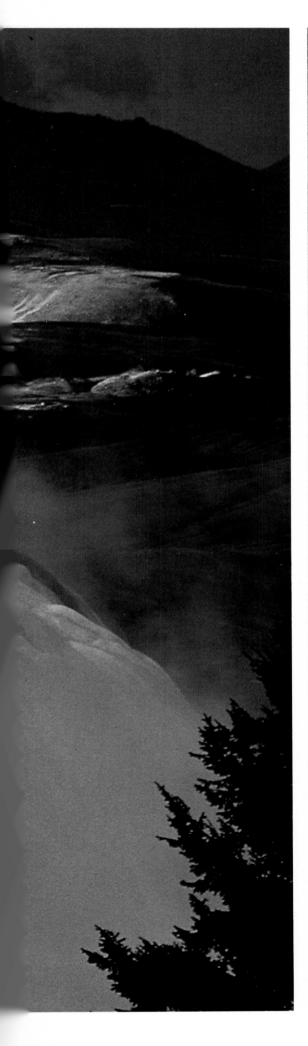

YELLOWSTONE COUNTRY

There has always been something special about the Yellowstone country, but its earliest native inhabitants hardly seemed awed by the spectacular scenery; they were more concerned with the earth's peculiar palpitations. "There is frequently heard a loud noise like thunder, which makes the earth tremble," they said. "They state" said an early explorer, "that they seldom go there because their children cannot sleep — and conceive it possessed of spirits, who were adverse that men should be near them." The Crow, Blackfeet, Northern Shoshoni, and Bannock all lived around this region and hunted through what is now the park — certainly their ancestors did, perhaps as much as five to ten thousand years before — but when the first Europeans came in search of furs, they found only a "timid and impoverished" band of the Shoshoni, known as "Sheepeaters", who had made a home there.

The white man seems to have skirted the Yellowstone basin in his early travels west; the Lewis and Clark expedition came close in 1804. John Colter, a member of that expedition, broke away on the return east and became the first known white man to see the wonders of what we now define as the park. He never wrote about it but he talked a great deal and, while at first many of his stories were discounted as exaggerations and just plain untruths, his name was left behind here just as it was in the Grand Tetons.

Between 1807 and 1840, the fur trade and reports of gold brought many Easterners into the country; but like the words of John Colter, their tales of boiling springs, geysers, mountains of glass, and other phenomena were given little credence. And so for another thirty years the Mi-tsi-a-da-zi, "the land of Rock Yellow Water" as the Sioux called it, remained little known to the public and something of a mystery. Trappers and hunters continued to come, and the "tall tales" lured the curious, but even the most eloquent journals were not convincing. The public wanted some proof, something official, and it came in 1870 in the day-by-day report of a young cavalry lieutenant, Gustavus Doane, who accompanied Henry Washburn, Surveyor-General of the Montana Territory, to "the falls and lakes of Yellowstone."

Doane was neither geologist nor writer, but he had a keen eye and a gift for description. He climbed what is now Mount Washburn, and he measured the height of the geysers, and he tried to describe what had happened geologically. "A single glance at the interior slopes of the ranges," he wrote, "shows that a former complete connection existed, and that the great basin has been formerly one vast crater of a now extinct volcano. The nature of the rocks, the steepness and outline of the interior walls, together with other peculiarities, render this conclusion a certainty." Doane was very nearly right, and his report became a classic.

Fortunately for the conservationists, it was one of those times in the history of America when things were going right for them. Thoreau's and Emerson's essays were being read, and conservationists were calling for preservation of the natural state of things. Thoreau wrote: "Why should not we ... have our national preserves ... in which the bear and panther and even some of the hunter race may still exist and not be 'civilized off the face of the earth' ... for inspiration and our true re-creation? Or should we, like villains, grub them all up for poaching on our own national domains?"

Washburn, whose expedition had consisted of some rather prominent people, led the march on Congress. Yellowstone, as yet untouched by the exploiters must be saved. The idea had been discussed during the expedition. "It was at the first camp after leaving the Lower Geyser Basin," wrote Cornelius Hedges, a lawyer and correspondent, "when all were speculating which point in the region we had been through would become most notable, when I first suggested uniting all our efforts to get it made a national park, little dreaming such a thing was possible." Yellowstone National Park was established on March 1, 1872.

Previous pages Yellowstone: a permanent mist hangs over the lip of the waterfall at Canary Springs.

Below In the Upper Geyser Basin is Yellowstone's most famous single feature: Old Faithful Geyser.

This page *Two scenes in the Grand Canyon of the Yellowstone: (right) the winding course of the river in the bed of the Canyon; (above) Yellowstone Falls.*

Fortunately for all, the creation of Yellowstone National Park came before western land exploitation reached into this high country, so we can only speculate what might have happened if it had. We know the wildlife was already endangered from hunting and trapping and remained so for a number of years after the park was formed. In fact, some species were nearly destroyed due to poor law enforcement. If gold had been discovered — and certainly it was sought — politics and economic interests would have been formidable forces with which to reckon. As it was, during the early years there were plenty of second thoughts about the two million acres set aside "as a public park or pleasuring-ground for the benefit and enjoyment of the people". Pressures on Congress were enormous: the timber, railroad, and cattle industries, to say nothing of those interested in mineral rights, and even the military, who claimed the Indians would never be subdued until their primary source of food, the buffalo, was destroyed. Congress wavered as individual members urged the government to get out of the tourist business and the raising of wild animals.

Only those who take time to see this park — and understand what they see — can appreciate the bargain Washburn and the others got for their time and trouble in 1870-72. Yellowstone National Park is nearly 3,500 square miles of virgin wilderness, land unchanged except by Nature itself. Less than 2 per cent of the total area has been affected by human intrusion. Not only is it the nation's largest wildlife preserve, it is a

Below *The Hayden Valley, Yellowstone — a piece of natural prairie that has been saved from modern land development.*

Above *The Teton Range, spectacularly illuminated in a winter sunset. Grand Teton National Park is a near neighbor of Yellowstone, only a few miles to the south.*

Right *Devil's Tower National Monument, Wyoming. This was once a column of molten lava in the "throat" of a volcano. After the eruption, wind and weather have eroded away the rest of the volcano, leaving the hard basalt exposed like the stump of a gigantic tree.*

Below *Close-up of the Devil's Tower. This formation is known as columnar jointing, caused by cracks formed due to shrinkage on cooling.*

geological wonderland unlike any other on earth — spouting geysers, bubbling mudpots, steaming fumaroles and pools of boiling water, hundreds of ponds and lakes surrounded by dense forests, rivers and streams rushing through black and yellow canyons, 8,000-foot plateaus, and 10,000-foot mountains; and populated throughout by bear, moose, elk, bison, wolves, coyotes, deer, antelope, dozens of other mammals, and hundreds of species of birds.

If we are to place an age on this land, it would be over 2.5 billion years; that's the age of the most ancient rock. But rather than repeat the story of the Rocky Mountain building, of which this is basically a part, it is more important to come forward to about 600 thousand years ago when the last of three great volcanic eruptions took place, and the caldera or crater that formed the Yellowstone basin. This chain of events has been estimated to be of mammoth proportions, unlike any in recorded times. Six hundred cubic miles of molten rock was thrown out onto the land. Clouds of volcanic ash buried entire forests. It must have been like all the geysers, mudpots, thermal pools, earthquakes — yes, there are tremors of some sort every day — happening at once on a scale a million times greater and for a long period of time. There are no adjectives to describe it all.

Then all was quiet ... all but the pot simmering just beneath the surface. It simmers still ... and you can see it, hear it, smell it. Is the age-old activity still dying away, or is it a renewal, or perhaps the birth, of some new fury that will one day, once more, alter this landscape?

Right *Morning Glory Pool hot spring, Yellowstone.*

Below right *Liberty Cap, the dry vent of a now extinct hot spring in Yellowstone.*

Below *Canada geese at dawn in Yellowstone.*

INDEX

Numbers in **bold type** refer to illustrations

PICTURE CREDITS

Ardea title, 14 top, 22, 22-23, 28-29, 29, 30, 31 bottom, 34-35, 36, 38 left, 42 inset, 43, 45, 52 top, 54-55, 57 top, 58-59, 66-67, 68, 70-71, 77 top, 77 bottom left, 77 bottom right, 79 bottom **Click/Chicago Limited** 9, Willard Clay contents, 18-19, 27, 63 top left, 63 bottom, 69 bottom, Tom Dietrich 56, Susan L Elkert 26, Warren Garst 70 **Bruce Coleman Limited** 8 bottom, 15 top, 16-17, 17 inset, 18 inset, 35, 36-37, 39, 40, 46-47, 49, 53, 58, 63 top right, 64, 64-65, 69 top, 74, 76, 78-79, 79 top **Creative Cartography** 10-11 **The Image Bank** Eddie Hironaka endpapers, Don Landwehrle 65, 72-73, Burton McNeely 62-63, J Netherton 60-61, Alex Stewart 20-21 **National Park Service** 6-7, 8 top, 12, 13 top, 14 bottom, 14-15, 24, 25, 31 top, 32-33, 52 bottom **Natural History Photographic Agency** 57 bottom **Spectrum Colour Library** half title, 13 bottom, 34, 38 inset, 40-41, 42, 44-45, 48, 48-49, 50, 51, 75 top left, 75 right

Front Cover: **Bruce Coleman Limited**
Back Cover: **Zefa**

Multimedia Publication (UK) Limited have endeavored to observe the legal requirements with regard to the suppliers of photographic material.